TIME AND THE WHITE TIGRESS

Books by Mary Barnard

Cool Country, 1940
A Few Poems, 1952
Sappho: A New Translation, 1958
The Mythmakers, 1966
Collected Poems, 1979
Three Fables, 1983
Assault on Mount Helicon, 1984
Time and the White Tigress, 1986

COLOPHON

Time and the White Tigress was set in Garamond 3. Garamond is one of a number of early twentieth century revivals of the typefaces of Jean Jannon of Sedan (c. 1610), which in turn were based on the mid-sixteenth century French typefaces associated with the name of Claude Garamond. Composition by Irish Setter.

The text is sixty-pound acid-free Warrens' Olde Style. The design is by Susan Applegate of Publishers Book Works and Patrick Ames.

The illustrations are specially commissioned linocuts by Anita Bigelow.

Time and the White Tigress was manufactured in April and May of 1986 by McNaughton & Gunn Lithographers, Inc. of Ann Arbor, Michigan.

One hundred copies have been numbered and signed by the author and the illustrator.

Illustrated by Anita Bigelow

TIME AND THE WHITE TIGRESS

Mary Barnard

BREITENBUSH BOOKS
Portland, Oregon

The author and publisher wish to express special appreciation to the Western States Arts Foundation and its corporate and public sponsors. The Western States Book Awards are a project of the Western States Arts Foundation. Corporate founders of the awards are The Xerox Foundation and B. Dalton Bookseller. Additional support is provided by the National Endowment for the Arts Literature Program.

First Edition 2 3 4 5 6 7 8 9 10

Library of Congress Cataloging in Publication Data
Barnard, Mary.
   Time and the white tigress
   Bibliography: p.
   1. Time—Poetry. 2. Mythology—Poetry.
3. Astronomy—Poetry. I. Title.
PS3503.A5825T54   1986   811'.52   85-31353
ISBN 0-932576-31-1
ISBN 0-932576-33-8 (pbk.)

Special gratitude is extended to the Oregon Arts Commission.

The author and publisher gratefully acknowledge permission to reprint the following: Section III of the Third Fytte, first published under the title "The Pleiades" in *The New Yorker*; "Song for the Northern Quarter," first published in *The Paris Review*; "Song for the New Year," first published in 1985 as a Christmas Broadside by the University Libraries, State University of New York at Buffalo.

Further acknowledgments go to Princeton University Press for permission to adapt the design of the Navajo Twin Heroes from a sand painting by Jeff King in *Where the Two Came to Their Father: A Navaho War Ceremonial*, Maud Oakes, ed., © 1943, renewed 1971 by Princeton University Press; to the University of California Press, Richard C. Rudolph and Wen Yu for permission to base two illustrations on material in *Han Tomb Art of West China* (Berkeley, 1951); and to the Pierpont Morgan Library for permission to base an illustration on a cylinder seal in possession of that library.

The medallion on the cover is taken from a Chinese roof tile now in the possession of the Metropolitan Museum of Art, with whose kind permission it is used. © 1986 by Anita Bigelow.

Designed by Susan Applegate and Patrick Ames. Illustrated by Anita Bigelow. Breitenbush Books are published by James Anderson.
Breitenbush Books, P.O. Box 02137, Portland, Oregon 97202-0137

To the Memory
of Three Women Astronomers

Maria Mitchell
Maud W. Makemson
Jessie M. Short

Maria, my collateral kinswoman
Maud, my friend and counselor
Jessie, my long-ago teacher

Fit, fytte *obs.* exc. *arch.* Some regard the word as identical with
OHG *fiza* list of cloth, mod. Ger. *fitze* skein of yarn, also
explained in the 17th c. as the thread with which weavers mark
off a day's work; the sense 'division or canto of a poem' might
well be a transferred use of this. . . .

O.E.D.

Contents

PROLOGUE

No society without customs
and with customs come ceremonies
(come feasting and dancing).
With ceremonies come calendars;
before calendars, sky-watchers.

They watch the sunrises moving along the horizon,
the moon with her arches low and then lofty, waxing
and waning, while both the sun and moon hold fast
to the tilted path of the Zodiac's twelve constellations.

The feasts and dances are held at new moon, at full moon,   10
whenever the sun stands still in the north or south,
and turns, and again when night and day are equal.
The watchers determine the day or night for feasting,
but not until time is measured, the beat established:
they split the year into halves and then into quarters.
They find the North and South and East and West.
They draw a cross in the sand. They watch the shadows,
the sun and moon, the rising and setting of stars,
and then they mime their knowledge:
                                        two dancers, first,   20
emerge from left and right, from east and west,
miming the laws that they have read in the skies.

1

I

The Year into Halves

I

In the beginning there were two, and they were Twins,
one dark, one light; horsemen and heroes,
physicians, shamans, and sons of God;
> virtuous
> beneficent
> devoted
> inseparable.

The Twins ranged widely, north as far as the Baltic,
south to the Punjab and Burma. Their constellations
rose over Greece and set over Italy. Carrying   10
with them a staff notched with the moon's divisions,
they crossed the steppes, the tundras, rambled through all
the Americas, and invariably they were a pair:
like eyes or hands, like feet or kneecaps or wings.

Wherever they went they carried two jugs,
one blue and one black, light and dark,
that measured the dripping water called time.

They were never sun and moon, but sons of the Sun
and Dripping Water, sons of the Moon as Changing Woman.

Sons of Leda and Zeus in the guise of a swan,   20
they hatched from an egg when day and night were equal.
They marked the birthplace of time, and divided the year.

They marked the crossing of three celestial highways,
the first called Path of the Dead, or Watling Street,
or River of Heaven (the galaxy's outer rim).
The second path is traveled by sun and moon,
passing, repassing, above and below, and finally
meeting squarely, the sun blacked out in eclipse.
The third is the path the stars take night after night,
intersecting obliquely the path of sun and moon.   30

They rose and set with these crossings, whatever the season;
and always one set as the other rose; one died
while his brother lived, and whenever the night sky cleared
one Twin or the other was bound to be visible
          rising due east
          setting due west
one Twin escorting the sun at the equinox
while the moon at its full went hand in hand with his brother.

          Their legends are beyond counting.

II

We are following here the spoor   40
of a White Tigress who prowled
Time's hinterlands once
in the Age of Dragons.

Her teats, dripping a moon-milk,
suckled the Twins. The savor,
still on our tongues, is fading.

Here, a pug-mark in the path.
There, bent grass where she crouched.
From this I construct a tigress?

A mythical one?   50
Perhaps. Why
should we cease to make myths?

III

The angle of the ecliptic
is like a door standing ajar;
its discovery, Pliny said,
opened the portals of science.

Upon that point, says Dante,
where two circles intersect

God's unwavering gaze is fixed,
it so inspires His love.   60

That angle formed the cleft
through which (at the equinox)
the poet stepped out of time
into timeless hell and heaven.

There, at the hour of sunrise
(the sun rising in that angle)
four circles make three crosses,
and light and dark are equal.

Crosses, crossroads, portals.
The stars that mark them guard   70
crossroad or gateway, being warriors,
archers, scorpion-men . . .

                         or Twins.

II

SECOND FYTTE

The Year into Quarters

I

The Fishes flicker, as Dante said—
    i Pesci guizzan su per l'orizzonta,
rising in our day with the sun at the equinox
(the vernal equinox, the birthday of time);
but long ago, when a Twin still guarded the crossing,
the Fishes rose with the Sun at the winter solstice.

Then or now, of all the Zodiacal twelve,
Pisces must be the silliest constellation;
we see two fishes swimming, one west, one north;
two strings extend from their tails to unite in a knot;   10
and among the quivering, flickering stars of Pisces,
all of them faint, the brightest one is the knot.

Ridiculous. Preposterous.

Or is it?
Here is the calendar-priest with his stake and his string,
the instruments of his art. We have his instructions:
"Level the ground. Erect your post or stake.
Mark the end of the shadow cast by the stake
three times during the day—any three times—
and call the three points *a* and *b* and *c*.   20

"Now take the string and draw an arc on the ground
using *a* as the center. Then, using *b* as the center,
describe a second arc intersecting the first.
The figure described by the pair of arcs intersecting
is known as a *fish*—in sanskrit, *matsya*.

"Now make a second fish with two additional
arcs drawn on the ground, one with *b* for a center
(again), and one with *c* for a center. Next
the string is drawn through the fishes' mouths and tails
in two straight lines, till they meet; then mark the join   30
(or knot), and draw a line from the knot or join
to the base of the stake. This line will tell us the where
and the when, the north and south, the hour of noon,
and show us the days when the sun turns back on its tracks.

"In the cross of the four directions, this line extended
becomes two arms, and points to North and South.
This line, joining Pole to Pole, is called the meridian
(the word is from *medi* and *dies*, midday, or noon).
Whenever the finger of shadow cast by the stake
crosses this line, whatever the day of the year,   40

the time of day will be noon. When the shadow at noon
is shortest, the day is the summer solstice; the sun
will turn south and his arches diminish. When the shadow
at noon is longest, the day is the winter solstice;
the sun once again turns north. By means of this line
we divide into equal halves the circle of time
(the year) and the circle of space as well—the horizon."

And here, in this figure described on leveled earth,
we have a pattern for Pisces: here are two fish
whose tails are tied by a cord outlining a V,   50
the crux of the problem solved by the point of the V,
the join, or knot, corresponding to *alpha Piscium*.

At the vernal equinox, at time's beginning,
when one Twin rose from the eastern hills at dawn
and his brother sank behind the hills in the west,
the Fishes were seen overhead (but south of the zenith).
The Knot in the cord would have marked the meridian. This,
I submit, is what we call Myth. Forget about Ovid.
His story of Venus and Cupid fleeing from Typhon
is pretty enough, but lacks both the cord and the knot.   60
The constellations were named by calendar-priests
whose tools were leveled ground, a stake, and string.

II

Opposite Pisces, Virgo. Across from the Knot,
Spica, a brilliant star, an ear of barley
held in the hand of Kore, daughter of Ceres
the Barley-mother.

                    Spicifera est Virgo Cereris.
An ear of wheat or barley—or is it instead
a barley *corn*?

                And what obscure tradition   70
has made the virgin a mermaid—a lascivious creature
by all accounts, like the Syrian Venus of Ashkelon?
Kore was never a mermaid, nor Astraea either
(Astraea, Goddess of Justice, holding the Scales).

At the autumn equinox, at Time's beginning,
when one of the Twins appeared on either horizon,
the Fish were below the earth, the Knot invisible.
Spica marked the meridian. The mermaid marked it.

We should remember about our calendar-priest
that he had two tricks up his sleeve.   80
                      With his stake and string
he could if he liked describe instead of two fish
a single figure that gave him his north-south line.
Sometimes he called it a fish (*matsya*), at others
a *barley corn*. Far-fetched? We think so, perhaps,
but only because it makes sense where we look for confusion.

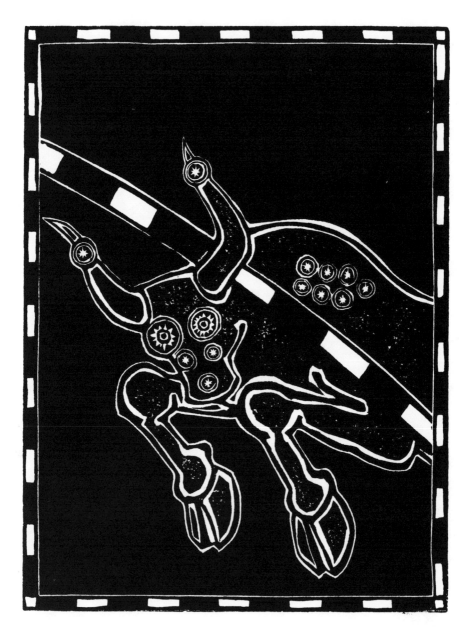

III

Time Slips a Cog

I

Out of the east the days march in single file,
all without name or number. From dawn to dark
today looks much like yesterday or tomorrow.
The night sky differs, marked by the moon's quick changes
from new to full to dark and back to new.
Nights will be named before days: the night of new moon,
full moon, night of no moon at all. We shall number,
first, the nights rounding out a lunation; later,
the days that make up a year. The moon-god, they say,
invented and taught mankind the science of numbers.   10

It must have happened like this: the lunar phases
marked first, and the round of seasons; a year count next;
then the twelve moons of the year were numbered—numbered

and named, with two full moons singled out from the others
and noted especially—moons that rose with the Twins
(the stars marking east and west, and spring and autumn).
These moons seemed always to linger, held at the full
longer than others—the autumn one rising at sunset
on several successive evenings; the other, opposite,
setting at sunrise for two or three nights in a row.   20
One need not be able to read and write to know this.

Harvest Moon, Easter Moon: one or the other rising
at twilight, setting at dawn, announced the year's end
and a new year's beginning, and through (how many?) milleniums
festivals clung and still cling to these moons shining
all night at the full when day and night are equal.

II

Nothing persists in the face of time and its flux
like the cultural off-shoots of time—calendar customs.
Mohammed knew, and trashed the solstitial year,
dislodged the sun from his count and exalted the crescent.   30
But aeons ago (in the age of the Twins) a schedule
once made was adhered to, a cycle of feasts once established
persisted; the lore of moon and stars handed down
from aforetime was sacred; changes were not to be thought of.
Not, at least, until time's own face had changed.

   Call them the Gemini People: nomads,
   perhaps. When the Harvest Moon was full

each autumn (the time and place of its rising
announced by a Twin on his fleet-footed steed)
they danced the Dance of the Dead. They mimed, 40
they mopped and mowed and painted their faces,
dancing in honor of those who had died
since the Harvest Moon last rose. All this
they did each year as their fathers had taught them.

The centuries passed, and the heavens changed.
The Harvest Moon kept pace with the seasons—
well and good; but the Twin that had risen
before it, announcing its coming, now
followed after the moon and off to the left.
The Moon of the Dead was now the full moon 50
rising between the horns of the Bull.

Mythology changed. Iconography changed.
The Pleiades, stars of the Bull constellation
joyously danced the New Year in,
dancing at dawn with the full moon of spring,
dancing at dusk with the full moon of autumn.

Their legends, too, are beyond counting.

III

They are heard as a choir of seven
shining voices; they descend
like a flock of wild swans to the water.   60

The white wing plumage folds,
they float on the lake—seven
stars reflected among the reeds.

Tonight the Seven Little Sisters,
daughters of the Moon, will come down
to bathe or wash their summer dresses.

They wear costumes of the seven
rainbow colors, they wear feather
mantles they can lift in sea winds

raised by their singing, and so rise   70
flying, soaring, until they fade
as the moon dawns; their voices dwindle

and die out in the North Woods, over
Australian bush, from Spartan
dancing grounds and African beaches.

They have returned to the sky
for the last time, and even
Electra's weeping over Troy is stilled.

What girl or star sings now
like a swan on the Yellow River?   80

IV

And how did Taurus, the Bull, get into the heavens?
Is there astronomy here? Or did sky-watchers *see* him
outlined in stars—the great glowing eye of Aldebaran,
V-shaped face, the Pleiades on his shoulder
(for they saw him head-on)?
                              Not very likely.

Is Taurus the snow-white bull that abducted Europa
and bore her to Crete? Aratos and Ovid said so.
And is he that other bull, too, whose golden horns,
according to Virgil, open the year—the Taurus   90
candidus auratis aperit cum cornibus annum?

So it would seem. However, the deified bulls,
as well as deities crowned with the horns of a bull,
are so many: Egypt's Apis and Mnevis and Sumer's
Anu, the Great Bull of Heaven, and Nannar the moon-god.
But ancient sky-watchers were, I surmise, not so much
worshipping cattle as watching the moon and planets
passing along the ecliptic, between the horns.

Sky-watchers, lacking a telescope, sight through rings,
or, like the Maya, two crossed sticks; they sight   100
through a forking twig, notched leaves of the palm or even
the horns of cattle. The horns, in any event,
are the most significant feature of this constellation.
The ecliptic still passes between them, though not the equator.
But back in the days—or nights—when Taurus rose
with the Harvest Moon at its full, the crossroads of heaven
passed through his horns and on to the Seven Sisters.

For two thousand years, from the rise of Egypt's kingdoms,
the earliest cities of Sumer and those of the Indus,
down through the building of Troy, and Newgrange in Ireland,   110
the equinox moved on its way through the Bull constellation
and finally entered the Ram. Then calendars were corrected—
sometimes—by decree of priest or king; but the folk,
still timing their holy days by the moon and stars,
ignored the shift in the heavens; their quarterly festivals,
All Souls and May Day, the Feasts of Imbolc and Lammas,
came down as the cross-quartered calendar. Do you believe this?
No, perhaps not; but the Pleiades say it is true.

IV

The Sun in the Well

I

Sun-worship, someone has said, goes with kingship. Rather,
the solar year goes with kingship, with organization,
with agriculture and irrigation and towns.
The folk, wherever they are—whether following game
or herding cattle, on plains, in valleys, on mountains—
can see the moon, its phase, its attendant stars.
But to name the day when the sun turns *ageyneward*—the solstice,
summer or winter—the calendar-priest needs a temple
or simply a gnomon enclosed for its own protection
in sacred precincts; and that will turn into a temple.   10

After the sun-watching priest has found out for certain
the length of his gnomon's shadow at midsummer noon,
and measured the angle between the two solstice points—

if he then moves north or south, his labor is wasted.
His work is all to do over. Reason enough
why calendars pegged to the sun are useless to nomads.

And a calendar pegged to the sun is pegged to the solstices—
northernmost, southernmost points of the spiraling journey
the sun makes twice each year from tropic to tropic,
and *that* he does because earth's axis is tilted,   20
providing the cycle of seasons, inspiring poets
to dream of a cycle of ages, from golden to leaden.

Without the tilt, we should see the sun coming up
due east each day, and shadows cast on a dial
would be identical day after day year-long.
The nights and days would be always equal in length
and the year would be at the spring forever and ever.
Such, we are told, was the case in the Golden Age
(in Saturn's reign) and such was the case in Eden
before Eve tasted the apple, and God in anger   30
commanded the angels to push earth's poles askew.
Then mankind first knew winter and work and illness,
but sages taught that eternal spring would return
(the axis, that is, would revert to its upright stance)
but slowly, slowly, and not for a very long time.

II

The orientation of temples and tombs
and dancing grounds, of huts and hogans
and stone-age graves is an endless theme.
Some, like the Pyramids, stand foursquare
to the cardinal points, but some are skewed   40
to solstice sunrises: Stonehenge faces
the summer, Newgrange turns to the winter.

We all know all about Stonehenge, and mainly
we know we know nothing; and having said that,
we all leap in and start guessing. Why not?

Call them the Hyperboreans, like Graves
and Diodorus Siculus. Building in wood,
rebuilding in stone, improving, perfecting—
a process that lasted for hundreds of years—
they labored to raise this temple to Time.   50

And what did they do there? We take it for granted
they watched the sun rise over the hele-stone
(between two hele-stones, if there were two).

But *something* surmounted the giant trilithon,
central of five. A sundisk in bronze?

Let me digress.
                One night a mouse
and a camel laid bets on which would first

see the sun. The confident camel looked east,
but the mouse, climbing up on his hump, looked west   60
and won when he saw the sun's first rays
illumine the highest peaks in the west.

None of us know. I think they faced west
and when the unrisen sun's first ray
lit gilded bronze, they clashed their cymbals
and shouted and danced the dance of the dragon.
I'd like to know, but it's fun not knowing.
Whatever they did, they must have been somehow
obsessed with *solstices*. Why? Oh why?

III

If you were standing at noon on midsummer's day   70
on that invisible line called the Tropic of Cancer,
the sun would be straight overhead; you and your gnomon
would cast no shadow at all. The ancients observed
the phenomenon, marking the spot.

                 And there were wells.
The ancients also observed that a well sunk here
would trap the sun in its depths on the longest day.
The sun would reflect from the water—an accurate method
of finding the solstice, and marking the spot on earth
above which the sun stood still and turned to the south.   80
And a well is a permanent fixture. It may last for ages.

The need for water protects it; it may become sacred
and old traditions will gather thickly around it.

There *were* such wells and they did not move. What moved
was the Tropic. This has nothing to do with Precession,
but just as the ancients surely observed Precession,
they must have observed the moving midsummer solstice.

They must have become aware that a well renowned
for trapping the sun on the longest day of the year
held nothing but shadows now, spring, summer, and winter.   90

The solstice sunrises marked by stone-age alignments
were also moving, the angle between them (summer
and winter) diminishing ever so slightly as both of them
moved toward East, and each other, and spring . . .
Someone seems to have noticed and wondered about it.
Would seasons of freezing and burning sometime give way
to spring the year round, a return of the Golden Age?
Did the Hyperboreans wonder and watch and measure?
Such engineers as they were, they might have done.

V

Time Standing Still

I

I am asked, "But why don't they come out even?"
(For example, the solar and lunar time-counts.)
An oversight, I explain, on the part of God.
But nothing in all this cosmic clockwork ever
will come out without some fraction remaining.

    It follows, then, that we count, we tinker,
    we count again: after twelve full moons
    the moon catches up with the sun. But no—
    she is falling behind and we count again
    on fingers, toes or beads or knotted string: 10
    we score on wood or bone, and we tinker.
    A dozen moons to the year, about—
but once in a while an extra, thirteenth moon.

The horseshoe crab knows well, the Nereids know
whenever the thirteenth moon is about to intrude.
The spawning rhythm responds to both moon and sun,
adjusting their disparate cycles—awaiting their union.

Time as a constant seeping away is at once
indistinct and unbearable, a thin high sound
never swelling or breaking, continuous to the world's end,   20
stretching our nerves like a bowstring.
                            Ebb without flow.

    But time-counts marked by a stamp of the foot
    release the string to be drawn again.
    A rhythm established by moon after moon,
    tide after tide, and year after year
    has formed a framework for all our cultures,
    a pattern of custom that echoes the pattern
    woven by time in the heavens. And so,
    like the horseshoe crab and nereid worm,   30
    we marked the thirteenth moon with a pause.

    Time was at rest. Behavior altered.
    The thirteenth moon was "lost" or unlucky.
    It might be a signal for abstinence, or,
    in some other culture, the New Year carousal
    might be prolonged for another lunation.
    The monarch, perhaps, remained in seclusion.

The thirteenth month is the thirteenth hollow log
in which the Moon was found, restored to life.

II

But this was a cumbersome calendar. Sooner or later   40
the lunar count gave way to the solar year.
The thirteenth moon remained as a handful of days
when time stood still, and the moon caught up with the sun—
a dozen days at the year's end; this was the epact,
an interregnum, when, through a twelve-day chink
in the calendar, beings from outside time slipped in,
when mummers paraded, chain-dancing from door to door,
when Father Liber was king and the servant was master.

Babylon counted eleven days in the epact—
five days of abstinence followed by six of feasting;   50
these occurred in the spring, when the New Year began.
But Christian Europe paused at the winter solstice
when nights were longest, the season of Rome's Saturnalia.

From Christmas Eve to the night of the Magi's visit,
Epiphany: these were days when time was at rest,
and all the things that turn like time on its axis,
cart wheels, mill wheels, spindles, must also rest.
No courts of justice were held, but during the Zwolfen
the Frauen rode through the night with their train of hounds.
This was the Yule, the turning-round of the year.   60

The stars of the Dipper, the Hindus said, were resting
(the Rishis, the Seven Sages who order the seasons).
Time paused; life paused, and then began again.

III

In Egypt the counting continued, and number took over.
Their years, cut loose from sun and moon, had an even
one dozen months, their months had thirty days.
The twelve-day epact dwindled to five: five days
outside the months, between one year and the next,
five days lost by the moon in a crap game: holy
festival days, birthdays of the five   70
children of Nut, the sky-goddess. Five days
outside time, which must—

                        apparently it simply must
have a stop.

Across the Atlantic, number became an obsession.
The Maya included among their elaborate time-counts
a year composed of eighteen twenty-day weeks
with five days falling between one year and the next,
an interval ruled by the snub-nosed pole-star god,
five days when, we are told, the Maya refrained   80
from combing or washing, and likewise from heavy labor
lest some evil befall them. Life, brought to a halt,
was held in abeyance until the time-gap was over,
and then began again, all new. All new.

But not in Islam. There the moon
is in the ascendant. The sun is nowhere.
Number is nowhere. There is no epact.
Twelve lunar crescents round out the year
whatever the season. The month of fasting,

the days of feasting slide through the solar year,   90
slipping against the circle described by the Dipper.

However, an infidel may yet wonder
whether the thirteenth moon has survived
in despite of Mohammed, not as a twelve-day epact—
not as a five-day pause—rather,
its somber spirit tinges the ninth
Islamic moon, Ramadán: the difficult month
of dawn-to-dusk fasting that ends in a three-day feast . . .

No time-count ever begins *all* new.

VI

Song for the Northern Quarter

I

The sun is a drum
               the moon is a cymbal
the flow of time is caught in a cup.

Cupful by
         cupful by
                  cupful time
is cut; if not,
               we should choke.

By night in the northern quarter the Dipper
or Northern Ladle or Bushel Measure   10
turns like the hand of a clock measuring time
although no punctuating tick or tock
notches its arc, sunset to sunrise.

Its handle divides the year into seasons,
pointing towards earth at dusk in autumn,
upward at dusk in spring, in winter
twilight west, in summer east.

And so it is and was and shall be
but not world without end (and neither
was it so from the world's beginning).   20

II

The stars of the northern sky revolve
in a circle dance, but slowly, slowly
(serpent mating with tortoise). The round
is a carol, revolving counter-clockwise
against the sun's apparent motion, as witches
turn with the left hand in, or withershins.

Instead of a ladle, instead of a dance,
a Bear: a lumbering she-bear nosing
the trunk of the cosmic tree. Or again,
the seven sages, the Hindu Rishis,   30
pace round the cosmic mountain. Instead
of any of these, it may be a plough.
It may be a thigh, or the leg of an ox.

It may be a carriage, a long-tongued cart.
Carol, carolus; it is Charles's Wain,

the cart of Carolus Magnus, Charlemagne.
And in China a chariot again, a triumphal car
for the pole-star god, Shang-ti, with winged attendants.

III

Praying, some face Mecca; some face the East,
the sunrise, the new day dawning, the future.   40
The Son of Heaven faced north, saluting the pole-star,
his double: the unchanging, unwobbling Center. Planets,
moon and sun and the stars that partner them
all pass from sight and return, but there at the axis
eternity is unmoved and out of time's reach.

This is the tent-pole of heaven, the shaman's tree
or the ash tree Yggdrasil. Or it may be a deity,
K'uei, for instance, the one-legged dancing master
who twirls on his single foot at the center of space
to set the stars in motion, and time's wheel turning.   50
Or Siva, dancing the dance of creation.

                          North
is more than cold. Wherever winter nights
are long and the Dipper wheels high in the sky,
too high for setting, the sovereignty of time
lies with neither sun nor moon: it dwells
in the mysterious core about which time turns.

VII

SEVENTH FYTTE

The Mating Serpents

I

Time has three distinct movements; the first is easy:
up and over and down from east to west
the sun and moon and stars careen together
as though on a giant wheel, riding its rim.
Darkness succeeds to light, and Yin to Yang.
That is the primary movement, east to west.

The second movement divides one year from another:
the sun moves backward along the rim of the wheel,
backward from spoke to spoke among the stars,
and a year has passed when the backward round is complete.   10
The moon, as well, moves backward along the rim
in the time (almost) of new moon to next new moon,
twelve times (about) to the sun's one backward round.

Some see the opposing movements as "good" or "bad,"
or the sun as willful, fighting against the stars,
or the sun as simply slow, and the moon still slower.

And then the third—a movement from north to south:
the heavens are seen as tilted, circling *their* pole
(hub of the wheel), as the stars go round and round;
but sun and moon dance round a different May-pole   20
and make a slanting passage among the stars.
They follow a path long ago y-clept th'ecliptic,
where sun and moon meet now and then in eclipse.

> *Three movements / three causes:*
> *First: earth turns on its axis.*
> *Second: earth orbits the sun.*
> *Third: earth's axis is tilted.*

II

Let us be clear about this: an eclipse of the sun,
an eclipse of the moon, are two quite contrary things.
The moon in eclipse is a full moon shadowed by earth;   30
her face is dulled; she is "sick," but visible still.
The sun and moon are on opposite sides of the earth.

An eclipse of the sun is much more dramatic and dangerous.
Month after month the moon overtakes the sun,
and, unseen in daylight, passes him by

above or below: but now and then they meet—
the moon's path crossing the sun's at a trysting place.
The two embrace, and we see the moon's black disk
surrounded by flames; but let the voyeur beware
of watching that copulation. Blindness can follow.   40

This is a total eclipse; the moon more often
contents herself with a bite from the rim of the sun.
These partial eclipses give rise to familiar tales
of monsters attacking and eating both sun and moon.
The monsters are various: toads and jaguars and snakes.
In the north we have Skoll and Hati, two hungry wolves,
the first pursuing the sun, the other the moon.
The gods were known to be doomed—the world would end—
whenever the Fenris wolf escaped from his chains
and swallowed both moon and sun. His head was a wolf's,   50
his body that of a dragon—serpentine.

III

The sky-watchers, tracking a three-fold motion
(the east-west movement of sun and moon,
their backward movement among the stars,
a to-and-fro motion from north to south
and south to north, solstice to solstice)
found that the paths formed coils, or spirals—
were serpentine—and drew two serpents
holding the sun and moon in their twig-like arms.

Eclipses occur on the lunar nodes;   60
and "node" is from *nodus*, "knot,"
the point where the sun's path crosses the moon's
and lovers join. The lunar nodes,
which are two, have ancient, significant names.
They are *caput draconis* and *coda draconis*.
Head of the Serpent, Tail of the Serpent
(or dragon). "Snake" in Greek is *drakon*.

An eclipse is then a conjunction of serpents,
the sport of a pair of celestial dragons,
a tryst of lovers, and more than this: 70
a beat in the longer rhythms of time.

Eclipses, we know, occur at predictable intervals.
Even in ancient times the rhythm was noted;
the watchers perceived, at least, that a cycle existed.
The imminent union of sun and moon was watched for,
observed as marking the end of a cycle, and feared
as possibly putting a period to time itself.
Warnings were issued and due precautions taken;
prayers were repeated and drums were beaten,
horns were sounded and fire-tipped arrows loosed at the sun.   80

And not in vain, for time has not yet ended.

VIII

EIGHTH FYTTE

The Jars

I

The sun by day, the moon and stars by night
display the elapse of time—if skies are clear.
The sundial's finger of shadow, telling the hours
on sunny days, is erased by rain and darkness.
Then what of the sentinel's watch on a foggy night?
How was it timed before the invention of clocks?

To measure the briefer intervals, day or night,
the ancients invented the *clepsydra*, "water-holder."
A clepsydra measures time by water descending
like sand in an hourglass. Two identical pots,   10
one filled with water that trickles out of a hole
to fill the other below it, are all we need.
A lawyer's speech was timed by a pair of cups;

amphoras, one for day and one for night,
measured the relative length of night and day,
and—most important—determined when these were equal.
The twin amphoras along with the stake and string
were primary tools for the earliest calendar-priests.

II

Time, then, was water flowing
cupful by brimming cupful . . .   20

Time was water dripping.
It dripped from a dragon's tongue
in Chinese gardens (a clepsydra
molded in dragon-shape
measuring the night hours—
                    plock! plock!).

Time dripped like spaced-out drops
falling in limestone caves,
with infinite slowness
building stalactites   30
like spikes of solidified time,
monuments, as it were,
to the passing milleniums.

Time has many faces
and some are the masks of God.

III

Time slipped a cog, as I have described.
The sun at the winter solstice, the moon
at her full in midsummer, deserted the Fishes
and moved to Aquarius, Water-Carrier
or Water-Pourer—a jar being emptied.   40
Astrologers called it the clock-makers' Sign.
The pot, to them, was half of a clepsydra
brimful of water. Summer or winter,
the longest day or the longest night
had filled it to overflowing. For once,
perhaps the astrologers' judgment was sound.
Or was it tradition? Who knows by now?

Water is life, and water is time,
and human life is a span of time:
a cup running over or emptied in death.   50

IV

The watering pot of Aquarius, pouring time,
is the only Zodiacal vessel of any description.
Nevertheless, the Gemini, Castor and Pollux,
are known in ancient art by a pair of amphoras
appearing sometimes beside them, sometimes alone:
identical jars, identical twins—twins who,

in the Gemini period, presided over the equinox,
jars that we know were used to determine the date.

Of the twelve Zodiacal figures, the Scales appeared last,
the symbol of balance replacing the Scorpion's Claws   60
as the equinox moved from the Pleiades to the Ram
and the full moon of spring rose opposite in the Scales.
Time means nothing unless it is measured. The Twins
with their stars and jars were earlier symbols of balance.
They signify the division of time into halves,
for they are the halves of an egg, the halves of the year,
the halves of a circle that runs from sunrise to sunrise.
Twice each year, midway between solstice and solstice,
the earth from pole to pole shares equal dark
and light. The Twins have ranged almost as far.   70

V

Time and space coalesce, of course. They must.
The organs of time define the quarters of space.
East is the rising-direction, west the setting.
Slow stars creeping around the pole spell north.
The sun at midday, south. Abstractions like these
need handles, a name, a color, a picture to tell us
this direction is east, this north. Let east
be green and south be red as in ancient China,
color north black and color west white. We may,
besides, incise a symbol in stone. Let west   80

be a tiger, south a bird and east a dragon,
the north a tortoise or serpent and tortoise mating.
    White Tiger
    Green Dragon
    Red Bird
    Black Serpent and Tortoise.
Then give the sun to East and the moon to West
(it is there the moon is born each month).
Give spring to East and the Dragon,
give autumn to West and the Tiger,   90
give summer to South and winter to North and at last
the universe is in order. We know where we are.
When we build our hogans and temples, or bury our dead
we know how to place them in space and in time.

And there we are, too, with four graven images
standing alert to gather power to themselves
and spring to life as Chiefs of the Four Directions—
doubled Twins pouring water (or wind or rain?)
from four identical jars. Bacabs, Chacs,
personified, deified quarters of space and time.   100

IX

La Donna

I

The moon is a woman, because it controls
a woman's flow of blood, or because
the moon is changeable, fickle, *mutabile*
or *mobile*; because its light is weak
compared to the sun's fierce rays (although
in eclipse the moon blacks out the sun).

The moon is a woman—not always, of course—
not in Japan; but let that pass.
For the most part she is a woman.
Perhaps because she is female the moon   10
has womanly skills—she spins and weaves.
Her spindle, potent for witches' spells,
turns, turns, turns in her fingers

spinning the thread of time, for time,
which is trickling sand, is also a thread.

Trivia, Hecate, or Triformis,
the goddess has three phases: crescent,
full and waning, and time three faces,
past, present and future. Whether,
in triple form, the spinner be time   20
or the moon, the thread she spins is life.

> *My thread is spun.*
> *My glass is run.*
> *My life is done.*
> *Go cause the bells to toll.*

II

La Donna has also the matronly skills
of a midwife. Mayan women in childbirth
cried out to Ixchel, a goddess wearing
a knotted snake in her headdress, weaving
her thirteen skeins of colored yarn   30
into time's intricate patterns. She,
like Peruvian Mamaquilla, like Brigit,
like mighty Diana diva triformis
(and heaven knows how many others)
is cast in the role of midwife for obvious reasons.
Nine lunar cycles will bring the child to birth.

She favors, la Donna, moisture, dew,
the sea whose tides dance to her measures,
and such shellfish and other sea creatures
as spawn by her calendar; rabbits are hers,   40
and night birds like the owl companion her.

III

Or, in another epiphany
she may be the Evening Star.

Appearing in early twilight
in the still-gilded western sky
she is the smiling planet
that leads young lovers to bed,
or she is reviled, hated and feared
as the treacherous, lecherous, feminine
force that is man's undoing.   50

Venus, Freya, Ishtar, Astarte:
the planet is never the goddess.
The brilliant, mysterious point of light
appearing and disappearing,
always keeping close to the sun,
is but one epiphany
marking the times of her ascendancy.

X

Song for the Millenium

I

If the world exists, it must have begun;
if the world began, it must come to an end. . . .

If time began, must it not end?
But when the beginning, and when the ending?
And may we not hope that when time ends,
it begins again, as a year will end
and a new year begin? We arrive in this fashion
at months of years and years of years
and ages of ages, sometimes likened
to reigns of kings: time's dynasties.   10

Meetings provide the divisions of time:
the coming together of moon and sun,

moon and star, planet and planet—
eclipses and occultation—all these
may serve to begin an age and foretell,
as well, the hour of its ending.

               Then Ixchel
draws a thread, for the fytte is finished.
She leaves her loom and Aquarius-like
empties her painted water-jar.   20
Her gesture brings the age to an end.

II

Five lesser lights, companions of moon and sun,
move along the ecliptic, backward (like them)
among the stars, but then (unlike the sun
or moon) reverse their motion, gain on the stars,
and finally, seeming to change their minds, drop back.
Because of these apparently whimsical movements,
the planets play only one role in calendar making.
They help to determine the longer cycles of time.

Imagine a primal conjunction of all five planets   30
and sun and moon lined up in their starting gates
at the hour of Creation, and set them all in motion.
The sun will have circled the course a dozen times
to Jupiter's once, providing our year of years.
Saturn, the slow old man, takes thirty years

to go around once, a "month of years" as they say;
personified, his image is with us still
as Father Time or the Old, departing Year.
But Venus, with her irregular comings and goings
takes over in Meso-America. There, her cycles   40
(his cycles, rather, for Venus there is a male)
determined the night when the Bundle of Years was tied,
when the sacred fire was extinguished, to be lighted again
in the heart of a human victim. End and beginning.

III

Time moves in a round.

              The moon and sun
appear to spiral around the earth,
passing among the stars that turn
like a wheel.

              The year is a ring   50
(*annus*, annular, annual)
that goes from spring to fall to spring
as the sun, leaving the Fishes,
circles around to the Virgin
and circles on until it returns
at the year's end to the Fishes.

As year is added to year the rings
expand; but always the coiling serpent
will have his tail in his mouth.
                    Cycles are circles.   60

"The gyres! The gyres!" cried Yeats
of time that moved in a circle
and played the same tune over
and over and over; but others
have held that the cosmic wheel,
reversing itself, will play time backward
whenever the Magnus Annus ends.

Thus the Great Year's seasons,
the ages of gold, of silver, of bronze,
of iron (the present) returning   70
in backward order will bring mankind
again to a Golden Age when winter
and war and pestilence are unknown.

The shepherd will pipe to his sheep
and the lion will lie down beside them.

IV

But, whether time is believed to proceed or turn back,
the end of an age is marked by a *kataklysmos*,
a Deluge. Then Ixchel's painted jug is emptied

and water flows in a stream from the serpent's mouth.
But some say the Hero Twins, smashing their jars,   80
released the water that washed away all of Creation.
Still others blame the Gods of the Four Directions,
the Bacabs (or doubled Twins) who caused the Flood
and later restored the universe to order.

Others elaborate on the theme: successive ages
are ended by earthquake, wind and conflagration;
however many the ages, however many
the forms of destruction, the end is seen in the heavens,
foretold by conjunctions of sun and moon and planets,
and, beyond these, by Precession. But even this,   90
the so-called Platonic Year, is dwarfed by cycles
the Maya imagined, and India's cosmic seasons,
wheels whose rims were measured in millions of years.

Or is time a spiral, circling but never repeating,
a spiral extending without beginning or end?
But endlessness we cannot comprehend.
As the vernal equinox moves to the Water-Pourer,
as another millenium comes to a close, we shiver
as we have always shivered, and hope as always.

Life runs on and runs out, and time runs on   100
and around, but measured by moons, by daylight and dark,
by tides that rise and fall, and by feet that dance.

CODA: *Song for the New Year*

The Pleiades slide into place
at midnight over the smoke-hole. . . .

A star that was lost in daylight
reappears at dawn (heliacal
rising) glittering in pale sky. . . .

The moon, too, dies in light
and returns at dusk, a crescent
signalling with sun and star
time at its turning-point.

Sea-kingdoms trumpet the news   10
through their winding shells,
but shepherds through ram's horns;
bells clang in the steeples.

Time now to empty our houses
of ghosts and the year's rubbish;
chain dancers prance through the streets
and turn into dragons; firecrackers
pop; steam-whistles shriek.

The event is both social and astral,
an end, but not final,   20
a beginning that will end:
a serpent with his tail tucked into his mouth.

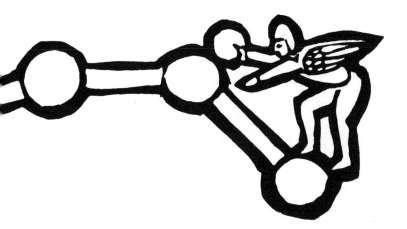

NOTES

Descriptions of astronomical phenomena in this poem are not designed to give the reader an explanation of the actual workings of the solar system as we now understand them. With one exception I have limited myself to descriptions of phenomena visible to the naked eye (i.e., to the ancient sky-watchers). My imaginary observers are viewing the heavens from somewhere in the north temperate zone. My account of the apparent movements of sun, moon and planets among the stars marking the ecliptic holds good for all parts of the earth, although the seasons are reversed in the southern hemisphere. The puzzled reader may consult any handbook of astronomy for clarification.

My volume of essays, *The Mythmakers* (1966), available from Breitenbush Books, gives a general background and bibliography for much of the material used in the poem, which is presented not as a work of scholarship, but as a work of imagination; however, I include a few notes for the reader who may be curious about my sources.

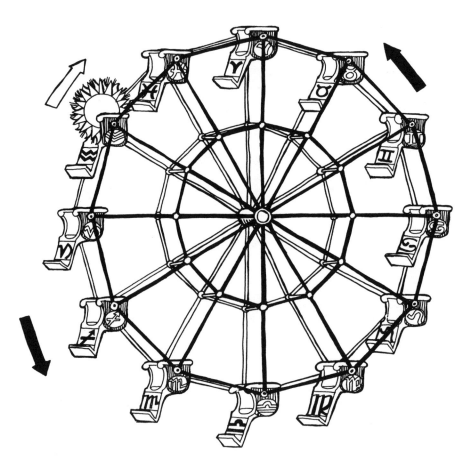

Figure 1. One thing must be kept in mind by the reader: the movement of the sun and moon among the stars is *backward*. Think of a Ferris wheel with twelve cars, each representing one Zodiacal constellation. The wheel turns steadily from east to west, completing a circuit in twenty-four hours. The sun travels east to west each day with the wheel, but at the same time it moves slowly backward from car to car so that it rides

once in each car in the course of a year. The moon also travels from east to west each night with the wheel, but moves backward from car to car so that it rides once in each car in the course of a month. When the moon rides in the same car with the sun, she is invisible (dark of the moon). When she is riding opposite the sun, the moon is full. The car (constellation) in which the sun is riding is always invisible, but the moon and the constellation can be seen together. This, combined with the moon's more rapid passage and changing phases, makes the moon more important than the sun in unsophisticated calendars.

FIRST FYTTE: *The Year into Halves*

For general background information see *The Mythmakers*, chap. 15, and authorities cited.

Lines 11-15 This is a staff described by Alexander Marshack in a lecture at the Smithsonian, 1983. He did not associate it with the Twins.

22-30 "At Time Zero, the two equinoctial 'hinges' of the world had been Gemini and Sagittarius. . . . The exceptional virtue of the Golden Age was precisely that the crossroads of ecliptic and equator coincided with the crossroads of ecliptic and Galaxy, namely in Gemini and Sagittarius . . ." Giorgio de Santillana and Martha von Dechend, *Hamlet's Mill* (1969), p. 63. This would have been the case for roughly two millenia, between 6000 and 4000 B.C.

53 The angle at which the circle of the ecliptic crosses the circle of the equator is approximately 23½°.

55-56 Pliny, *Natural History*, Book II, vi.

57-60 Dante, *Paradiso*, X. 7-12.

67 Dante, *Paradiso*, I. 39.

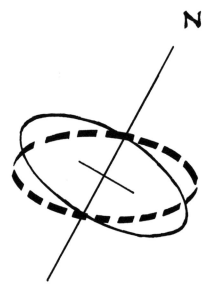

Figure 2. Diagram of ecliptic and equator with axis indicated. The broken line indicates the ecliptic.

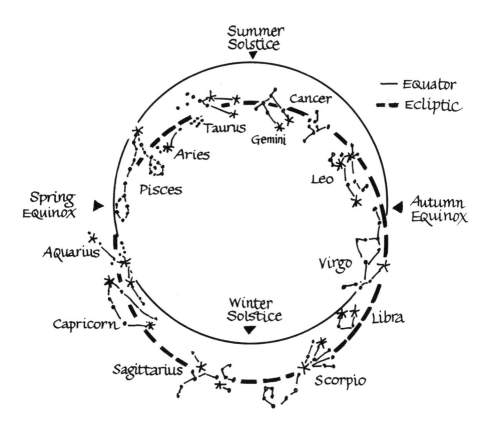

Figure 3. Diagram of ecliptic and equator with Zodiacal constellations indicated. The constellations are shown in the positions they now occupy.

SECOND FYTTE: *The Year into Quarters*

Lines 1-2 Dante, *Inferno*, XI. 113.

15 The promulgation and regulation of a calendar is normally a priestly function, among the Pueblo Indians as among the Egyptians and in most parts of the world. Our present calendar (the Gregorian) was promulgated by Pope Gregory XIII in 1582, and its predecessor, the Julian, by Julius Caesar as Pontifex Maximus of the Roman Republic in 44 B.C. The names, number, length and order of our months are those of the Julian calendar, but incorporating a few changes made under the Empire.

17-47 The text paraphrased in these lines is from *The Panchasiddhantika* by Varaha Mihira (sixth century A.D.), ed. and tr. by G. Thibaut (Lahore, 1930), chap. 14, stanzas 14, 15, and 19. See also G. R. Kaye, *The Astronomical Observatories of Jai Singh* (Calcutta, 1918), p. 78.

59-60 Ovid, *Fasti*, Book II. 458-474.

67 Manilius, *Astronomica*, II. 442.

81-85 Varaha Mihira, *op. cit.*, chap. 4, stanza 19.

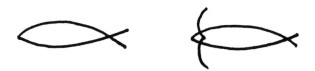

Figure 4. Fish pictograms. The one on the left is North American Indian, the one on the right is Egyptian. From A. C. Moorhouse, *Writing and the Alphabet* (London, 1946), p. 8, fig. 3.

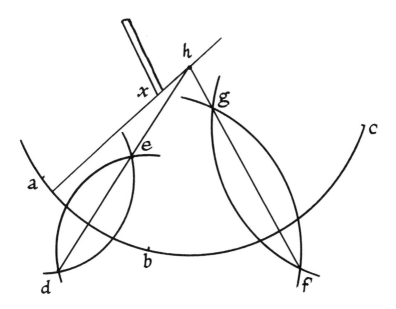

Figure 5. Diagram showing how to find the meridian according to instructions in the *Panchasiddhantika*. *x* is the gnomon. *h* is the knot. Points *a*, *b*, and *c* were believed to lie on the circumference of a circle, as shown here, although actually they do not.

THIRD FYTTE: *Time Slips a Cog*

In this fytte I am dealing with the phenomenon called Precession of the Equinoxes. See any astronomical handbook for the scientific explanation. However, one thing must be stressed: to an astronomer the Zodiac is an abstract circle of 360° divided into twelve segments of 30° each. The segments (called Signs) bear the names of constellations that coincided with them more than two thousand years ago, but not now. This does not confuse astronomers in the least. It need not bother the reader too much because I am referring in this work *always* to the constellations unless I use the word *Sign*. I am writing about a time before the abstract 360° circle had been devised. The same stars remain on the ecliptic, but the vernal equinox moves through the twelve constellations in about 26,000 years. In Cicero's day the cycle was estimated at 30,000 years.

Lines 14-20 For an explanation of the unusual behavior of the full moon at the equinoxes, see an astronomical handbook. For further background to this fytte, see also chapters 12 and 13 in *The Mythmakers*.
   91 Virgil, *Georgics*, I. 217.

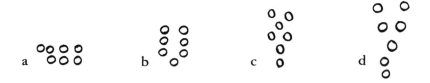

Figure 6. The Pleiades as depicted by the Babylonians (*a*, *b*), the Navajo (*c*), and Blackfoot Indians (*d*). The Pleiades are always referred to and depicted as seven, although only six are visible to the naked eye, and the placing of the seventh varies. At one time all seven stars were visible and many myths account for the disappearance of the seventh.

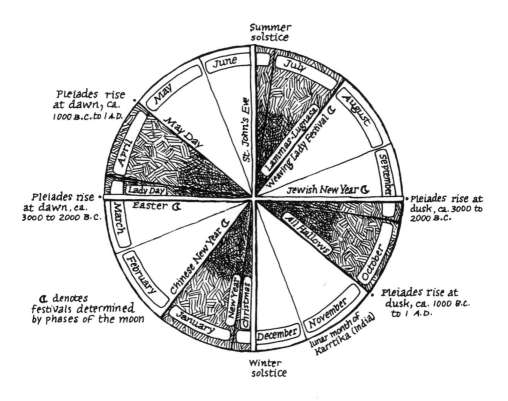

Figure 7. Diagram showing the equinoctial and solstitial holidays and those of the cross-quarters.

Fourth Fytte: *The Sun in the Well*

Lines   1 Mircea Eliade in *Patterns in Comparative Religion*, tr. R. Sheed
(New York, 1958), pp. 124 and 150.

28-29 See, for instance: Hesiod, *Works and Days*, lines 110-120;
and Ovid, *Metamorphoses*, I. 89-112.

29-32 Milton, *Paradise Lost*, X. 668-671.

42 Newgrange: a large passage-grave in County Meath dated to
ca. 3100 B.C.

47 Diodorus Siculus, *History*, II. 47.

54-55 The lintel of the central trilithon of the inner horseshoe (see
Figure 10) has fallen along with one of the uprights. Two
man-made depressions, as if for the placement of some super-
structure, are visible on what was once the top of the lintel.
Their existence is unexplained. See R.J.C. Atkinson, *Stone-
henge* (1956).

57-62 See Uno Holmberg, *Siberian Mythology* (1927), p. 437. In
this fable the mouse and the camel were vying for the honor
of opening the year, that is, of leading the list of twelve
animals in the Asiatic Zodiac.

84-85 The moving tropics are caused by "a very slight cyclical
change in the inclination of the earth's equatorial plane to the
plane of the orbit. It has a period of about 40,000 years . . ."
Atkinson, *op. cit.*, p. 86.

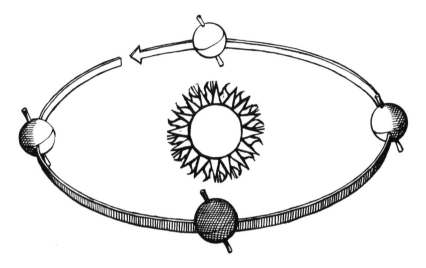

Figure 8. The earth with its axis inclined at an angle to the plane of its orbit, which causes summer and winter.

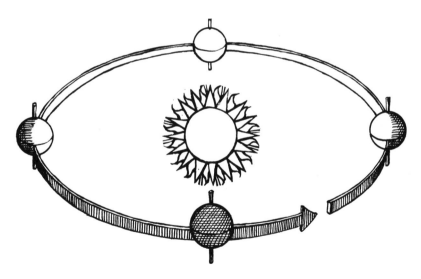

Figure 9. The earth with its axis upright as Milton realized that it would have been in a Golden Age when spring lasted all year long.

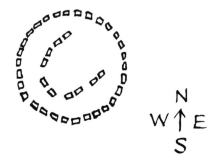

Figure 10. Diagram showing placement of the upright sarsen stones at Stonehenge. Those in the outside ring were joined by a continuous ring of slightly curved stone lintels. The larger uprights forming the horseshoe were joined in pairs by five lintels to form five "trilithons." The central trilithon was the tallest (24 ft.).

FIFTH FYTTE: *Time Standing Still*

On the lunisolar spawning cycles, see *The Mythmakers*, chap. 10, and authorities cited; also Rachel Carson, *The Edge of the Sea* (1979), pp. 34-36.

Lines 38-39 J. Eric Thompson mentions this tale in his monograph, "The Moon Goddess in Middle America" (1934).

    42-53 The actual length of the epact varies slightly from year to year, hence the length of the interregnum varies between eleven days as in Babylon, and twelve days as in western Europe. For examples of the interregnum, see Mircea Eliade, *The Myth of the Eternal Return* (1954). On the Babylon festival, see Stephan H. Langdon, *Babylonian Menologies*

(1935), p. 107. The latter cites a tablet of the seventh century B.C. which "states distinctly" that the eleven days of the festival are a supplement to the lunar year. In Brittany the twelve days of Christmas were known as the *gourdeziou* or supplementary days. For examples of customs and superstitions associated with the twelve days of Christmas, see Hutton Webster, *Rest Days* (1916), and Clement A. Miles, *Christmas in Ritual and Tradition, Christian and Pagan* (1912).

64-98 For the Egyptian, Mayan and Muslim calendars see the article "Calendars" in the *Encyclopedia of Religion and Ethics*.

73-84 Sahagun, quoted by Sylvanus Griswold Morley, *The Ancient Maya*. Revised by G. W. Brainard, 3rd ed. (1956).

SIXTH FYTTE: *Song for the Northern Quarter*

Lines 19-20 Precession also causes the aspect of the northern sky to change during the millenniums.

39-45 On the importance of the north-south axis in Chinese culture, see Ernst Zinner, *The Stars Above Us*, tr. Johnston (New York, 1957).

SEVENTH FYTTE: *The Mating Serpents*

For the mythology of lunar and solar eclipses, see *The Mythmakers*, chap. 11, and authorities cited.

Lines 38-39 Because the moon is much smaller than the sun, if it were any farther from the earth, it would move across the face of the sun without eclipsing it; on the other hand, if it were closer, we should be unable to see the corona. As it happens, the moon is at precisely the right distance to cover the sun without covering the corona.

52-54 Bear in mind that I am describing the way the sun and moon *appear* to move. The earth is actually orbiting the sun, while the moon orbits the earth.

58-59 For examples see Richard C. Rudolf, *Han Tomb Art of West China* (1951).

EIGHTH FYTTE: *The Jars*

Lines   13 Martial refers to a long-winded speaker who would have pleased everyone if he had wetted his throat from the clepsydra. *Epigrams*, VI. 36. Caesar's legions, like the Chinese armies, used the clepsydra to regulate the length of night watches.

19 The Romans had a phrase, *aquam perdere*, literally, "to lose water," figuratively, "to waste time."

22 Chinese clepsydras were usually ornamented with a dragon's head which spit water into the lower vessel. A poem by Hueh Feng (ca. 845 A.D.) mentions such a water clock.

34-35 With a bow to Joseph Campbell.

41 Robert Eisler, *The Royal Art of Astrology* (1946), p. 107.

59-64 Virgil (Georgics, I. 208-209) refers to Libra, which brings the hours of day and night into balance, *et medium luci atque umbris iam dividit orbem*—divides the world (*orbem*, sphere) in half between light and shadow. In ancient China, the autumn equinox was the time when instruments for weighing and measuring were to be adjusted. *The Li Ki*, tr. James Legge (Oxford, 1879-85).

71-100 On the colors and animals of the four directions and four quarters of the year, see chap. 13 of *The Mythmakers* and authorities cited.

NINTH FYTTE: *La Donna*

See *The Mythmakers*, chap. 3, and authorities cited.

Lines   7-8 The lunar deity is male in Japan, and the sun is female. Several mythologies, including those of Sumer and Egypt, seem to have had both male and female lunar deities.

16-20 For the Triple Goddess, see Robert Graves, *The White Goddess* (1948), *passim*.

27-31 Thompson, *op. cit.*, 133-134.

52 Robert Chadwick in a lecture at the Smithsonian, 1983.

TENTH FYTTE: *Song for the Millennium*

My sources include the article entitled "Ages of the World" in the *Encyclopedia of Religion and Ethics*; Mircea Eliade, *The Myth of the Eternal Return* (1954); W. B. Yeats, *A Vision* (1925) on the Platonic Year or Magnus Annus, which he also mentions in a number of his poems, especially "The Gyres."

Lines 35-38 The planet Saturn was assimilated to the Greek God Kronos. The scythe of Father Time was originally the sickle with which Kronos castrated his father Uranos.

39-44 A good discussion of the Mayan Venus cycles can be found in the new translation of the *Popol Vuh* by Dennis Tedlock (New York, 1985).

50-56 In a sense the year is the prototype of all circles, for in our geometry the 360° of a circle are derived from the 360-plus days of a year.

70 In any system of ages descending from good to bad, the present age is always the worst.

76-84 See *The Mythmakers*, chap. 14, and authorities cited.

All diagrams and line drawings are the work of Anita Bigelow. I am also indebted to Garry Stasiuk for his generous response and assistance in matters astronomical.

LIST OF ILLUSTRATIONS

TITLE A tiger representing the direction West, from *Han Tomb Art of*
PAGE *West China*, by Richard C. Rudolph and Wen Yu (Berkeley, 1951). Plate 72.

I   The Navajo Twin Heroes as depicted in the sand paintings of Jeff King. Child Born of Water is on the left, Monster Slayer on the right. From *Where the Two Came to Their Father*, by Jeff King (Princeton, 1969). Plate X.

II   The constellation Pisces. Design based on a number of representations, European and Arabic.

III   The constellation Taurus. Design based on various star-charts and traditional representations.

IV   Stonehenge. An original design.

V   Horseshoe crab and moon. Design inspired by the Tarot Greater Trump, *La Lune*. In astrology the Sign of Cancer (the Crab) is ruled by the moon.

VI   Serpent mating with tortoise, sometimes called the Black or Dark Warrior, Chinese symbol of the Northern Quarter. From *Han Tomb Art of West China* (see above). Plate 74.

VII   Sun serpent and moon serpent. An original design on the caduceus motif.

VIII   Twin jars representing the Dioscures as shown on a coin of Lacedaemon. Schwabe, *Archetype und Tierkreis* (Basel, 1951).

IX   The goddess Ishtar as she is depicted on a cylinder seal from Mesopotamia now in the Pierpont Morgan Library. The seal has been identified as belonging to the period of the new Assyrian

Empire and dated to the eighth or ninth century B.C. From *Mesopotamian Art in Cylinder Seals of the Pierpont Morgan Library*, text by Edith Porada (New York, 1947).

X   Ixchel emptying her water jar. Adapted from representations of the lady in the *Codex Dresdensis* and elsewhere. See *Latin American Mythology*, by Hartley Burr Alexander (Boston, 1920). Plate XXII.

Notes   The Big Dipper as depicted on a relief from the Wu Liang tomb shrine. China, *ca.* 147 A.D. The eighth star—the one held up by a winged figure standing on the end of the Dipper handle—represented the star Alcor, which is so close to its neighbor Mizar that they have been known as horse and rider, mother and child, or husband and wife (the lost Pleiad). From Edouard Chavannes, *La sculpture pierre en Chine* (Paris, 1893). Plate XXXII.

The above illustrations are all linocuts by Anita Bigelow.

Mary Barnard is a poet, translator, and essayist who lives in Vancouver, Washington. She was born in 1909 and attended Reed College. Her poems, essays, and fiction have appeared in *Harper's Bazaar*, *The New Yorker*, *The New Republic*, *The Paris Review*, *Kenyon Review*, *American Scholar*, *Northwest Review*, and the *Partisan Review*, among others. Her *Collected Poems* won the Elliston Award in 1979.

The companion volume to *Time and the White Tigress* is *The Mythmakers* (nonfiction).

Books by Mary Barnard available from Breitenbush:

The Mythmakers:
$12.95 cloth, $6.95 paper

Collected Poems:
$8.95 paper

Three Fables:
$4.95 paper

($1.00 postage and handling)

Breitenbush Books
P.O. Box 02137
Portland, Oregon 97202-0137